GERALD BARRY

The Chair

FOR ORGAN

The Chair was commissioned by the Dublin International Organ and Choral Festival 1994.

Cover illustration: watercolour by Gerald Barry

Oxford University Press, Walton Street, Oxford OX2 6DP, England
Oxford University Press, 200 Madison Avenue, New York, NY 10016, USA

Music Department
OXFORD UNIVERSITY PRESS
Oxford and New York

The Chair

Gerald Barry

𝅗𝅥 = 92 *brilliantly, with detached articulation*

Printed in Great Britain
OXFORD UNIVERSITY PRESS, MUSIC DEPARTMENT, WALTON STREET, OXFORD OX2 6DP

21
25
29
33

Chorale
♩ = 100
mp
mp

59
64
68
73

𝅗𝅥 = 92
77
81
86
91

96
5
100
106
111

116
120
123
127

130
ff
136
5
5
ff
140
145

151
156
160
164

169
5
5
173
177
5
5
5
180

184
Dance
♩ = 208 bouncing, detached articulation
189
sempre ff
196
202

208
214
219
♩. = 152 *with great rhythmic drive*
223
228

233
237
242
247
Add Reeds 8′, 16′
252
257

262
267
272
277
283

289
Chorale
295 ♩ = 100 sadly
mp
mp
299
303

307
♩ = 104
ff
ff
310
accel.
314
♩ = 144
319

323
328
Dance
bouncing
332
335
339
sim.

344
348
sim.
354
359
362

366
370
373
377

* indicates a chromatic cluster

393
396
399
402

*This passage may also be played at the slower tempo of ♩ = 138

Music origination by Barnes Music Engraving Ltd., East Sussex
Printed in Great Britain by Halstan & Co. Ltd., Amersham, Bucks.